Belongs to:

_____

Deer # _____

Date

Time

Season

Antler Points

☐ Doe or Antlerless

Weight

Weapon

Ammunition

Important Factor

Location & Terrain

Weather Conditions

This is what happened...

What I learned:

Deer # _____

Date	
Time	Weapon
Season	Ammunition
Antler Points	Important Factor
☐ Doe or Antlerless	
Weight	

Location & Terrain

Weather Conditions

This is what happened...

What I learned:

Deer # _____

Date

Time

Season

Antler Points

☐ Doe or Antlerless

Weight

Weapon

Ammunition

Important Factor

Location & Terrain

Weather Conditions

This is what happened...

What I learned:

Deer # _____

Date

Time

Season

Antler Points

☐ Doe or Antlerless

Weight

Weapon

Ammunition

Important Factor

Location & Terrain

Weather Conditions

This is what happened...

What I learned:

Deer # _____

Date

Time

Season

Antler Points

☐ Doe or Antlerless

Weight

Weapon

Ammunition

Important Factor

Location & Terrain

Weather Conditions

This is what happened...

What I learned:

Deer # _____

Date

Time

Weapon

Season

Ammunition

Antler Points

Important Factor

☐ Doe or Antlerless

Weight

Location & Terrain

Weather Conditions

This is what happened...

What I learned:

Deer # _____

Date

Time

Season

Antler Points

☐ Doe or Antlerless

Weight

Weapon

Ammunition

Important Factor

Location & Terrain

Weather Conditions

This is what happened...

What I learned:

Deer # _____

Date

Weapon

Time

Ammunition

Season

Antler Points

Important Factor

☐ Doe or Antlerless

Weight

Location & Terrain

Weather Conditions

This is what happened...

What I learned:

Deer # _____

Date

Time

Season

Antler Points

☐ Doe or Antlerless

Weight

Weapon

Ammunition

Important Factor

Location & Terrain

Weather Conditions

This is what happened...

What I learned:

Deer # _____

Date

Time

Season

Antler Points

☐ Doe or Antlerless

Weight

Weapon

Ammunition

Important Factor

Location & Terrain

Weather Conditions

This is what happened...

What I learned:

Deer # _____

Date

Time

Season

Antler Points

☐ Doe or Antlerless

Weight

Weapon

Ammunition

Important Factor

Location & Terrain

Weather Conditions

This is what happened...

What I learned:

Deer # _____

Date	**Weapon**
Time	**Ammunition**
Season	
Antler Points	**Important Factor**
☐ Doe or Antlerless	
Weight	

Location & Terrain

Weather Conditions

This is what happened...

What I learned:

Deer # _____

Date

Time

Season

Antler Points

☐ Doe or Antlerless

Weight

Weapon

Ammunition

Important Factor

Location & Terrain

Weather Conditions

This is what happened...

What I learned:

Deer # _____

Date

Time

Season

Antler Points

☐ Doe or Antlerless

Weight

Weapon

Ammunition

Important Factor

Location & Terrain

Weather Conditions

This is what happened...

What I learned:

Deer # _____

Date

Time

Season

Antler Points

☐ Doe or Antlerless

Weight

Weapon

Ammunition

Important Factor

Location & Terrain

Weather Conditions

This is what happened...

What I learned:

Deer # _____

Date

Time

Weapon

Season

Ammunition

Antler Points

Important Factor

☐ Doe or Antlerless

Weight

Location & Terrain

Weather Conditions

This is what happened...

What I learned:

Deer # _____

Date

Weapon

Time

Ammunition

Season

Antler Points

Important Factor

☐ Doe or Antlerless

Weight

Location & Terrain

Weather Conditions

This is what happened...

What I learned:

Deer # _____

Date

Time

Season

Antler Points

☐ Doe or Antlerless

Weight

Weapon

Ammunition

Important Factor

Location & Terrain

Weather Conditions

This is what happened...

What I learned:

Deer # _____

Date

Time

Season

Antler Points

☐ Doe or Antlerless

Weight

Weapon

Ammunition

Important Factor

Location & Terrain

Weather Conditions

This is what happened...

What I learned:

Deer # _____

Date

Weapon

Time

Ammunition

Season

Antler Points

Important Factor

☐ Doe or Antlerless

Weight

Location & Terrain

Weather Conditions

This is what happened...

What I learned:

Deer # _____

Date

Time

Season

Antler Points

☐ Doe or Antlerless

Weight

Weapon

Ammunition

Important Factor

Location & Terrain

Weather Conditions

This is what happened...

What I learned:

Deer # _____

Date	Weapon
Time	Ammunition
Season	
Antler Points	Important Factor
☐ Doe or Antlerless	
Weight	

Location & Terrain

Weather Conditions

This is what happened...

What I learned:

Deer # _____

Date

Weapon

Time

Ammunition

Season

Antler Points

Important Factor

☐ Doe or Antlerless

Weight

Location & Terrain

Weather Conditions

This is what happened...

What I learned:

Deer # _____

Date

Time

Season

Antler Points

☐ Doe or Antlerless

Weight

Weapon

Ammunition

Important Factor

Location & Terrain

Weather Conditions

This is what happened...

What I learned:

Deer # _____

Date

Time

Season

Antler Points

☐ Doe or Antlerless

Weight

Weapon

Ammunition

Important Factor

Location & Terrain

Weather Conditions

This is what happened...

What I learned:

Deer # _____

Date

Time

Season

Antler Points

☐ Doe or Antlerless

Weight

Weapon

Ammunition

Important Factor

Location & Terrain

Weather Conditions

This is what happened...

What I learned:

Deer # _____

Date

Time

Season

Antler Points

☐ Doe or Antlerless

Weight

Weapon

Ammunition

Important Factor

Location & Terrain

Weather Conditions

This is what happened...

What I learned:

Deer # _____

Date

Time

Season

Antler Points

☐ Doe or Antlerless

Weight

Weapon

Ammunition

Important Factor

Location & Terrain

Weather Conditions

This is what happened...

What I learned:

Deer # _____

Date	Weapon
Time	Ammunition
Season	
Antler Points	Important Factor
☐ Doe or Antlerless	
Weight	

Location & Terrain

Weather Conditions

This is what happened...

What I learned:

Deer # _____

Date

Weapon

Time

Ammunition

Season

Antler Points

Important Factor

☐ Doe or Antlerless

Weight

Location & Terrain

Weather Conditions

This is what happened...

What I learned:

Deer # _____

Date

Time

Season

Antler Points

☐ Doe or Antlerless

Weight

Weapon

Ammunition

Important Factor

Location & Terrain

Weather Conditions

This is what happened...

What I learned:

Deer # _____

Date

Weapon

Time

Ammunition

Season

Antler Points

Important Factor

☐ Doe or Antlerless

Weight

Location & Terrain

Weather Conditions

This is what happened...

What I learned:

Deer # _____

Date

Time

Season

Antler Points

☐ Doe or Antlerless

Weight

Weapon

Ammunition

Important Factor

Location & Terrain

Weather Conditions

This is what happened...

What I learned:

Deer # _____

Date

Time

Season

Antler Points

☐ Doe or Antlerless

Weight

Weapon

Ammunition

Important Factor

Location & Terrain

Weather Conditions

This is what happened...

What I learned:

Deer # _____

Date

Time

Season

Antler Points

☐ Doe or Antlerless

Weight

Weapon

Ammunition

Important Factor

Location & Terrain

Weather Conditions

This is what happened...

What I learned:

Deer # _____

Date

Time

Season

Antler Points

☐ Doe or Antlerless

Weight

Weapon

Ammunition

Important Factor

Location & Terrain

Weather Conditions

This is what happened...

What I learned:

Deer # _____

Date

Time

Season

Antler Points

☐ Doe or Antlerless

Weight

Weapon

Ammunition

Important Factor

Location & Terrain

Weather Conditions

This is what happened...

What I learned:

Deer # _____

Date

Time

Weapon

Season

Ammunition

Antler Points

Important Factor

☐ Doe or Antlerless

Weight

Location & Terrain

Weather Conditions

This is what happened...

What I learned:

Deer # _____

Date

Time

Weapon

Season

Ammunition

Antler Points

Important Factor

☐ Doe or Antlerless

Weight

Location & Terrain

Weather Conditions

This is what happened...

What I learned:

Deer # _____

Date

Time

Weapon

Season

Ammunition

Antler Points

Important Factor

☐ Doe or Antlerless

Weight

Location & Terrain

Weather Conditions

This is what happened...

What I learned:

Deer # _____

Date

Time

Season

Antler Points

[ ] Doe or Antlerless

Weight

Weapon

Ammunition

Important Factor

Location & Terrain

Weather Conditions

This is what happened...

What I learned:

Deer # _____

Date
_____

Time
_____

Season
_____

Antler Points
_____

☐ Doe or Antlerless
_____

Weight

Weapon

Ammunition

Important Factor

Location & Terrain

Weather Conditions

This is what happened...

What I learned:

Deer # _____

Date	Weapon
Time	Ammunition
Season	
Antler Points	Important Factor
☐ Doe or Antlerless	
Weight	

Location & Terrain

Weather Conditions

This is what happened...

What I learned:

Deer # _____

Date

Time

Season

Antler Points

☐ Doe or Antlerless

Weight

Weapon

Ammunition

Important Factor

Location & Terrain

Weather Conditions

This is what happened...

What I learned:

Deer # _____

Date

Time

Season

Antler Points

☐ Doe or Antlerless

Weight

Weapon

Ammunition

Important Factor

Location & Terrain

Weather Conditions

This is what happened...

What I learned:

Deer # _____

Date
_____

Time
_____

Season
_____

Antler Points
_____

☐ Doe or Antlerless
_____

Weight

Weapon

Ammunition

Important Factor

Location & Terrain

Weather Conditions

This is what happened...

What I learned:

Deer # _____

Date

Time

Season

Antler Points

☐ Doe or Antlerless

Weight

Weapon

Ammunition

Important Factor

Location & Terrain

Weather Conditions

This is what happened...

What I learned:

Deer # _____

Date

Weapon

Time

Ammunition

Season

Antler Points

Important Factor

☐ Doe or Antlerless

Weight

Location & Terrain

Weather Conditions

This is what happened...

What I learned:

Deer # _____

Date	Weapon
Time	Ammunition
Season	
Antler Points	Important Factor
☐ Doe or Antlerless	
Weight	

Location & Terrain

Weather Conditions

This is what happened...

What I learned:

Deer # _____

Date	Weapon
Time	Ammunition
Season	
Antler Points	Important Factor
☐ Doe or Antlerless	
Weight	

Location & Terrain

Weather Conditions

This is what happened...

What I learned:

Deer # _____

Date	Weapon
Time	Ammunition
Season	
Antler Points	Important Factor
☐ Doe or Antlerless	
Weight	

Location & Terrain

Weather Conditions

This is what happened...

What I learned:

Deer # _____

Date

Time

Season

Antler Points

☐ Doe or Antlerless

Weight

Weapon

Ammunition

Important Factor

Location & Terrain

Weather Conditions

This is what happened...

What I learned:

Deer # _____

Date

Time

Weapon

Ammunition

Season

Antler Points

Important Factor

☐ Doe or Antlerless

Weight

Location & Terrain

Weather Conditions

This is what happened...

What I learned:

Deer # _____

Date

Time

Season

Antler Points

☐ Doe or Antlerless

Weight

Weapon

Ammunition

Important Factor

Location & Terrain

Weather Conditions

This is what happened...

What I learned:

Deer # _____

Date

Weapon

Time

Ammunition

Season

Antler Points

Important Factor

☐ Doe or Antlerless

Weight

Location & Terrain

Weather Conditions

This is what happened...

What I learned:

Made in the USA
Las Vegas, NV
10 November 2023